LEONARDO DA VINCI

In the 1460s, Florence (a city in what is now Italy) was one of the most important places in Europe, and the rich men of the city had money to spend. It was a good place for an artist, because rich men wanted paintings and sculptures for their great new homes.

In the workshop of the artist Andrea del Verrocchio, the apprentices worked hard, making paint, cutting stone, drawing and finishing paintings. One young apprentice was different from the others. He studied things carefully and asked questions about them. He learned from Verrocchio, from the other apprentices, and from the world around him. And soon the world would know the name of Leonardo da Vinci – one of the greatest painters and thinkers of all time.

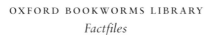

OXFORD BOOKWORMS LIBRARY

Factfiles

Leonardo da Vinci

Stage 2 (700 headwords)

Factfiles Series Editor: Christine Lindop

ALEX RAYNHAM

Leonardo da Vinci

OXFORD UNIVERSITY PRESS

OXFORD
UNIVERSITY PRESS

Great Clarendon Street, Oxford, OX2 6DP, United Kingdom

Oxford University Press is a department of the University of Oxford.
It furthers the University's objective of excellence in research, scholarship,
and education by publishing worldwide. Oxford is a registered trade
mark of Oxford University Press in the UK and in certain other countries

ISBN: 978 0 19 423670 6

A complete recording of *Leonardo da Vinci* is available on CD. Pack ISBN: 978 0 19 423662 1

Printed in China

Word count (main text): 7,033

For more information on the Oxford Bookworms Library,
visit www.oup.com/elt/gradedreaders

ACKNOWLEDGEMENTS

Cover image: Alamy Images (Self portrait of Leonardo da Vinci/Leo Macario)

The publishers would like to thanks the following for permission to reproduce images: Alamy Images
cover (Self portrait of Leonardo da Vinci/Leo Macario); Bridgeman Art Library Ltd pp.5 (*Woman
looking down*/British Museum, London, UK), 007a (*The Lady with the Ermine*/Czartoryski Museum,
Cracow, Poland), 17 (*Studies of the coronary vessels*/The Royal Collection 2011 Her Majesty Queen
Elizabeth II), 29 (*An Acrobat and Wrestlers Performing*, 15th century/Ashmolean Museum, University
of Oxford, UK), 41 (*A study of a woman's hands*/The Royal Collection © 2011 Her Majesty Queen
Elizabeth II); Corbis pp.008a (*The Last supper* by Leonardo da Vinci/The Gallery Collection/Corbis),
10 (Horse in profile/Derek Bayes – Art/Lebrecht Music & Arts), 13 (*Mona Lisa* by Leonardo da
Vinci/The Gallery Collection), 16 (*Vitruvian Man* by Leonardo da Vinci/Bettmann), 18 (Armoured
Tank designed by Leonardo da Vinci on display in Hangzhou/WU HONG/epa), 26 (Diving suit/
James L. Amos), 31 (*The Madonna and Child with Saint Anne* by Francesco Melzi/Christie's Images),
37 (Clos Luce Mansion/David Brabyn), 38 (Leonardo Da Vinci statue/Tetra Images), 39 (Statue of
a horse/Ocean), 44 (Medieval battle re-enactment/Jim Richardson/National Geographic Society),
44 (ASIMO robot/Splash News), 44 (Statue of a horse/Ocean); Getty Images pp.32 (Anatomical
studies/Hulton Archive), 34 (Santa Maria della Grazie/Leonardo da Vinci), 44 (Castle/Buena
Vista Images); Kobal Collection p.33 (*The Da Vinci Code*/Columbia); Oxford University Press
pp.44 (Painting/Corbis), 44 (Workshop/James Hardy); Press Association Images p.20 (Parachute/
Laurent Gillieron/AP); Rex Features pp.28 (*The Musician* by Leonardo da Vinci/KeystoneUSA-
ZUMA), 35 (Da Vinci's Workshop/Sipa Press); Robert Harding World Imagery pp.0 (Cathedral
of Santa Maria, Florence/Roy Rainford), 2 (Vinci, city of Leonardo/age fotostock), 14 (Fossil/
CuboImages), 50 (Florence, Tuscany, Italy/Stefano Cellai); Science Photo Library p.23 (Leonardo's
plan for canals in a town/Sheila Terry); The Art Archive pp.24 (*Atlantic Codex*/Leonardo da Vinci/
DeA Picture Library/Metis E Mida Informatica/Veneranda Biblioteca Ambrosiana), 27 (Cesare
BORGIA, 1475–1507/Accademia Carrara Bergamo Italy/Collection Dagli Orti).

CONTENTS

1   Leonardo da Vinci

It is a winter afternoon in 1467, and the artist Andrea del Verrocchio is walking along a busy street in Florence. On both sides of the road, people in workshops are making glass, pictures, beautiful clothes, and many other things. From an open door he hears the sounds of people at work, cutting stone and hitting metal.

Andrea stops and goes through a door into his workshop. It is noisy inside, and it smells of smoke and chickens. A big fire is burning and everyone is busy. At one end of the room, he sees Leonardo – a tall, good-looking boy with long hair. He is the son of Andrea's friend, Ser Piero da Vinci.

Leonardo is fourteen years old. He has only been in the workshop for about a year, but Andrea is very happy with him. He is a clever boy: he works hard and he learns fast. What is he doing when Andrea comes in? Perhaps he is breaking eggs to make paint. Does he turn around and smile?

Today we remember Leonardo as a famous painter and a great thinker. We are still studying his work and learning new things 500 years after his death. Surprisingly, the great Leonardo da Vinci did not come from a rich family, and he did not spend much time at school. So how did he become one of the cleverest and most famous people in history?

2   Early life

Leonardo was born on 15 April 1452 near a small town called Vinci. The family name 'da Vinci' just means 'from Vinci'. The town is built on a hill about 35 kilometres from Florence, but in 1452, that was a long day's ride by horse. Vinci was a quiet town, far away from the great buildings, money, and important people of Florence.

Leonardo's mother and father both married different people after he was born. His father, Ser Piero da Vinci, lived and worked in Florence, but his mother, Caterina, stayed in Vinci. Leonardo probably spent most of his early life around Vinci.

The town of Vinci

Leonardo knew a lot about life in the country. He played in the fields around the town, and he loved animals. Leonardo watched the workers and he learned how people built and made things. He was interested in everything, and he soon began to draw.

Leonardo could not go to school with the children of important families because his father and mother were not married. At the time, many books were in Latin, but because Leonardo did not learn this language at school, he could not read them. Years later, he finally taught himself to read Latin.

When he was young, Leonardo had to teach himself other things too, like how to write. Leonardo wrote with his left hand, and he used mirror writing, which is very difficult to read. When you put a mirror next to his writing, you can read it. He learned to draw with his left hand too.

Mirror writing

When Leonardo was about thirteen, his father took some of his drawings to a friend in Florence – the artist Andrea del Verrocchio. Verrocchio liked the drawings, and in about 1466, Leonardo became an apprentice – someone who learns new things while he works – in Verrocchio's workshop. Leonardo enjoyed drawing, so he was very happy!

Verrocchio's workshop was like a small factory, and lots of people worked there. The workshop made many different things, like beautiful paintings and sculptures, and clothes for important days of the year. Leonardo probably started with small jobs, like making paint or cleaning the workshop. Later, he learned to draw, work with stone, design clothes, and do many other things.

The apprentices lived above Verrocchio's workshop. They ate, laughed, and played music together. The boys became great friends, and sometimes they fought. For Leonardo, it was like a new family.

In workshops like Verrocchio's, lots of people worked on the paintings. Verrocchio did the most important work, and then his best apprentices finished it. Leonardo was a fast learner, and he soon became a talented painter. Before long, he was helping Verrocchio to finish important paintings.

At the time, Italy was made of lots of different small countries. Florence was the biggest city of one of these countries. It was also one of the biggest and richest cities in Europe. People were building churches and great houses all over the city, and they needed paintings and sculptures to put in them. It was a time of new ideas about painting, science, and many other things. Today, we call this time 'the Renaissance'.

Because Florence was a very rich and important city, it was home to many of the greatest thinkers and artists of the time. Some of these great men visited Verrocchio's workshop, and the young Leonardo met them. He probably dreamed that he could be like them too. Florence in the 1460s was a great place for talented people – and nobody was more talented than Leonardo.

A drawing by Verrocchio

3 Painting and sculpture

There is a story about Leonardo when he was a young painter. One day, Leonardo was finishing a Verrocchio painting in the workshop when Verrocchio came in. Leonardo's work was beautiful, and Verrocchio knew it. 'I'll never paint again,' the older man said. Leonardo was not an apprentice any more – he was one of the best young painters in Florence.

Most workshops at the time used a paint that was made with eggs, but Leonardo tried a new paint – oil paint. It was possible to do more things with oil paint, and it helped him to paint deeper, brighter colours. Leonardo went outside and drew things like flowers, water, and stones. He studied these things like a scientist. He also worked with doctors to understand how our bodies work. Because of this, everything in his pictures was very real.

Leonardo's father helped him to open a workshop in Florence, but it was not an easy time for Leonardo. He had a lot of problems with some important people. In 1482, Leonardo left Florence and travelled to Milan. Leonardo left angry people behind him back in Florence, because he had not finished paintings for them. This happened all through his life. Leonardo is one of the most

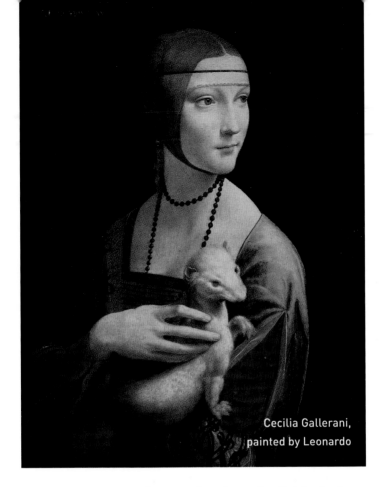

Cecilia Gallerani,
painted by Leonardo

famous painters in history, but he only finished about twenty paintings! This painting of Cecilia Gallerani is one of them.

Leonardo was happy in Milan. He had a busy workshop with lots of young apprentices. The ruler of Milan, Ludovico Sforza, spent a lot of money on art because he wanted to show that he was as good as the rulers of places like Florence. Leonardo was given money to be a part of Sforza's court – the circle of important people who worked for him. He designed buildings and machines for Sforza. He also painted beautiful pictures, like the painting of Cecilia Gallerani – Sforza's young love.

In 1495, Sforza asked Leonardo to paint a picture called *The Last Supper*. The painting was for the wall of an important church building, and it told the story of the last meal Jesus had with his followers. It took Leonardo many months to plan the picture. He drew each person and changed how they sat or stood around the table. Leonardo's design for the painting is amazing. The lines of the walls in the real room are the same as the lines in the picture: it is like

looking into another part of the same room.

The Last Supper is a very big painting, 4.6 metres tall and 8.8 metres long, and it is on a very high wall. People built places for Leonardo to stand while he worked. Sometimes, he worked for hours and did not stop to eat. At other times, he stood and looked at the painting for hours, but he did not touch his paints.

Leonardo finally finished *The Last Supper* in 1498. It was one of the greatest paintings of the Renaissance, but Leonardo was worried. When he painted *The Last Supper*, he worked in a different way from most painters, and he made the paint in a different way too. Soon, he

The Last Supper

understood his mistake. The painting started to break into pieces. When Leonardo looked at his great work, he probably thought, 'It will fall off this wall in a few years.' Luckily for us, people found ways to save it.

At the same time as *The Last Supper*, Leonardo was working on a great sculpture of Ludovico Sforza's father Francesco. Leonardo wanted to make a sculpture of Francesco on a great horse. For years, he drew horses and made designs, but there were problems. Leonardo made sculptures when he worked with Verrocchio, but this sculpture was much bigger. He wanted it to be the biggest sculpture in Europe, and he needed about 60 tonnes

Horse drawings by Leonardo

(60,000 kilograms) of an expensive metal called bronze to make it. His drawings show a walking horse with only two legs on the ground, but how could he put a heavy sculpture like this on two legs?

In 1492, Leonardo made a great horse sculpture in clay. It was 7.3 metres tall and it was amazing. People talked about the clay horse for years, but Leonardo never made the final metal sculpture. Why? Because the bronze for the horse was used to make guns. There was a war between France and Milan, and in 1499, Ludovico Sforza had to leave the city. When the French army arrived, French soldiers shot at Leonardo's clay horse and broke it into pieces. After seventeen years in Milan, Leonardo left the city.

When Leonardo was fifty-two, the rulers of Florence asked him to paint a picture of a famous battle for a great building in their city. On the opposite wall, they asked Michelangelo to paint another battle. The two men were enemies. Michelangelo was only twenty-nine, but he was already famous for his amazing sculptures. One day, he laughed at Leonardo in front of people in a town square. He said that Leonardo was not a good artist, because he could not build his great horse.

Both men worked on their paintings, and it soon became a battle between the two most famous artists of their time. Who was the best? Everyone in Florence talked about them and waited to see their great works, but in the end neither of them won the battle. Michelangelo made some drawings, but then he went back to Rome. Leonardo started his painting, but because of the way he painted on the wall, it soon began to break into pieces.

At about the same time as he was working on the battle painting in Florence, Leonardo began a painting of a young woman called Lisa del Giocondo. Today we call it the *Mona Lisa*, or *La Gioconda*. Leonardo used new ideas to paint the *Mona Lisa,* and other painters soon began to work in this new way.

But is that why it became the most famous picture in the history of art?

Look at Mona Lisa's face. Is she starting to smile? Now look again – she is not smiling any more. We look from one side of her mouth to the other, and her smile changes in front of our eyes, like the smile of a real person. What is she thinking? Because of that smile, you stop and look at the painting again. You ask yourself questions. Writers like Emile Zola and Oscar Wilde wrote about Mona Lisa's smile. They said she was a dark and dangerous woman: her smile hid many secrets.

On 21 August 1911, a man called Vincenzo Peruggia walked into the Louvre Museum, in Paris. He took the *Mona Lisa* off the wall, put it under his coat, and walked out of the building. The next day, the *Mona Lisa* was in newspapers around the world. When the museum opened again, thousands of visitors went to see the empty place on the wall! For two years, Peruggia kept the painting in his house in Florence. He hid it in a box under some old clothes. Peruggia was caught in 1913 when he tried to sell the painting, and the *Mona Lisa* then came back to Paris. But nobody forgot the story of the lost woman with the strange smile.

Today you can find the *Mona Lisa* in paintings by modern artists, on clothes, in films and songs, and a thousand other places. Leonardo usually painted important people, but Lisa del Giacondo was not famous. She was just a young wife from Florence, but she became one of the most famous women in the world.

Opposite page: *Mona Lisa*

4

Into the dark

One day when Leonardo was a child, he was walking near Vinci and he found a deep, dark hole in the side of a hill. He wanted to look inside, but he was afraid of the dark. It was better to walk away, but Leonardo was curious – he had to go in.

Leonardo was one of the most curious men in history. He was full of questions, and he wanted to know the answers. He wanted to learn how our bodies work, how the weather changes, what the moon is made of, and many other things. He thought deeply, studied the world around him, and discovered things for himself.

When Leonardo was working for Sforza in Milan, he studied the rivers, mountains, and rocks of Northern Italy. He discovered how a lot of rocks are made by water over a very long time. High in the mountains, Leonardo also found fossils of animals that came from the sea. He asked, 'How did they get there?'

A fossil from Italy

In Leonardo's day, people thought that the things around them, like mountains and seas, always stayed the same. But the fossils told a different story. Leonardo discovered that the world around us changes over time. He wrote about how places under the sea can become mountains. It was an amazing idea for his time – and we did not know that he was right for hundreds of years!

People in Leonardo's day thought that the moon was bright because it made light. Leonardo discovered that the moon is bright because of light from the sun. Leonardo imagined that he was standing on the moon and looking back at the world. 'From the moon our world looks bright too,' he thought. And 450 years later, we finally photographed our world from the moon: a bright, blue circle in the dark, just like Leonardo imagined.

In Milan, Leonardo started to write about things like maths, painting, and engineering. His pages are full of beautiful drawings, with notes all around them. He often wrote about different things on the same piece of paper. Perhaps Leonardo did this because paper was so expensive at the time. Or perhaps he did it because he had so many ideas in his head – he could not stop thinking about different things.

In 1487, Leonardo made a drawing called the *Vitruvian Man*. It was made to study the body, and it has become the most famous drawing in the history of art. Today you can see it on €1 coins and in many other places. At the same time, Leonardo was making beautiful drawings of our anatomy – the inside of our bodies. Many people in Leonardo's day thought that it was wrong to study our

anatomy, but for Leonardo, the body was like a machine. He wanted to see how it worked. He studied how people were different from animals, and he worked with doctors. Leonardo cut bodies open, drew them, and made some amazing discoveries.

One day, Leonardo spoke to a very old man in a hospital in Florence. A few hours later the man died. Leonardo wanted to know why people die, so later he cut the man's body open and tried to find the answer. Leonardo saw that the walls of the man's arteries were much narrower than the arteries of a young person. 'Perhaps these narrow arteries stop the blood which is moving through our bodies,' Leonardo thought. Was he right? Did this problem kill the old man? We do not know, but about 25 per cent of all deaths today happen because of problems with the arteries and heart.

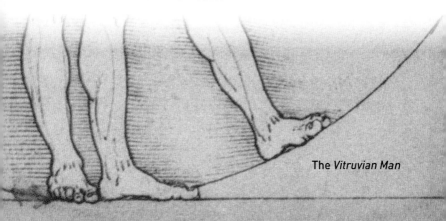

The *Vitruvian Man*

Amazingly, Leonardo's anatomy drawings are still helping people today. In 2005, a doctor at Papworth Hospital in Cambridge, England, studied Leonardo's drawings of the heart. They gave him an idea about how to work in a different way on one part of the heart. This helped to save people's lives.

It was not easy to study anatomy in Leonardo's time. He used knives and his hands to open bodies, and he often worked at night. The bodies began to smell bad very quickly, and at times Leonardo had to leave them in his workshop. It was hard to go into a dark room and look at death in the middle of the night. Leonardo was afraid, but he was curious too – he had to go and see.

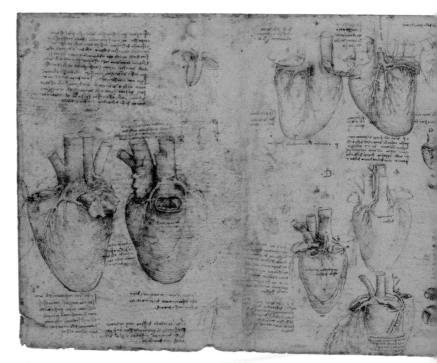

Anatomy drawings by Leonardo

5   The great inventor

In November 2011, visitors played with big wood and metal models in a shopping centre in Adana, Turkey. They turned and moved things, took photos, and read about the life of Leonardo da Vinci. The thirty-four models were made from Leonardo's drawings, and they showed machines for building things, studying the weather, flying, and even walking on water!

In Leonardo's time, people used machines to do things like move water or heavy stones. He learned to use and mend machines when he was an apprentice in Verrocchio's workshop. Leonardo studied these machines carefully and thought about different ways to use their parts.

A model of Leonardo's tank

Leonardo invented new machine parts and drew plans for many new inventions. He designed terrible guns, and machines that could cut wood, or make paint or books. He also invented musical instruments. Leonardo made one instrument from silver. It sounded beautiful and it looked like a horse's head!

Some of Leonardo's most famous inventions are his robots. They worked like the parts in a clock. They could move around a room for a short time without any help. Leonardo built different robots to entertain people at parties. One robot was like a car with three wheels. Once he built a robot soldier. It looked like a real person, and it could walk, move its arms, legs, and head, and open and close its mouth. Hundreds of years later, robot engineers in America have learned from Leonardo's robot designs. The drawings have helped them to build robots that look and move like people.

In 1485, Leonardo designed a parachute, but it was 515 years before anyone tried his design. In 2000 a British man called Adrian Nicholas made a jump with a parachute that used Leonardo's design and materials from his time. And in 2008 Olivier Vietti-Tepa from Switzerland made a jump of about 600 metres with a parachute that used Leonardo's design but modern materials. Both parachutes worked.

When Leonardo was in his fifties, he thought about his early life and wrote about it. What did he remember first? It was not his mother or father – it was a bird. When he was a baby, the bird flew down to him, and he never forgot it. Leonardo loved birds. He often bought birds

Leonardo's parachute
passes a helicopter

from people in markets, but he did not keep them. He paid the money and took the birds. Then he opened his hands, and the birds flew away free.

For years, Leonardo studied how birds fly. He dreamed of flying for most of his life, and he drew lots of different flying machines. One drawing shows a machine with turning wings. Leonardo's machine could not work, but nearly 400 years later, a young Russian boy called Igor Sikorski saw the drawing. He was a dreamer too.

After years of trying, in 1939, Sikorski built and flew a helicopter, the VS-300. Four years later, his factory was the first in the world to make helicopters.

Another drawing shows an ornithopter – a flying machine with wings that moved up and down like a bird. A pilot used his arms and legs to move the wings. In Leonardo's time, it was not possible to build this machine because the materials were too heavy. Finally, in 2010, students in Canada built and flew an ornithopter. It was made of very light materials, and the pilot moved the wings up and down with his legs.

In about 1505, Leonardo studied the wind on a hill near Florence, and he also wrote about flying from there. So the big question is 'Did he ever try to fly?' At the time, Leonardo and Michelangelo were planning their pictures for the 'great battle'. Both men wanted to show that they were the best. Was Leonardo planning to fly and show the world that he was cleverer than Michelangelo?

Thirty years after Leonardo died, a man called Girolamo Cardano wrote about how Leonardo 'tried to fly, but could not'. Cardano's father was Leonardo's friend, so was it true? There is nothing about it in Leonardo's writing, so we do not know the answer, but we can imagine it. We can see him on a hill near Florence on a hot summer day in 1505. He is standing and looking at the fields below, with his long hair moving in the wind. He puts on his wings. What is he feeling? He has dreamed of flying all his life, and now it is time to try. He could die, but he has to know the answer. He runs into the wind as fast as he can.

6   Leonardo's city

In the terrible winter of 1485, thousands of people became ill in the city of Milan and many died. Then on 16 March, the sky became dark in the middle of the day. People in the streets did not know what was happening – they probably thought that it was the end of the world. Scientists like Leonardo knew that the moon was moving in front of the sun. Leonardo made holes in a piece of paper to watch it. The sun did not hurt his eyes, because he held the paper in front of his face.

In just three years, about a third of the people in Milan died. Leonardo looked at the city around him, with its dirty canals and narrow streets, and he began to draw plans for a better, cleaner city. Leonardo's city had big streets and large open squares. He drew machines for moving water to workshops and houses, and he studied ways to keep the water clean.

Some of Leonardo's drawings show a city on two levels. The bottom level was for canals and roads, so horses, boats, and workers could bring things in and out of the city. On the top level, people could walk about. Many buildings had doors on both levels. In some plans, the canals and streets went under the buildings. Leonardo's city was never built, but parts of many modern cities are built on different levels.

In Leonardo's time, the centre of Milan was inside a

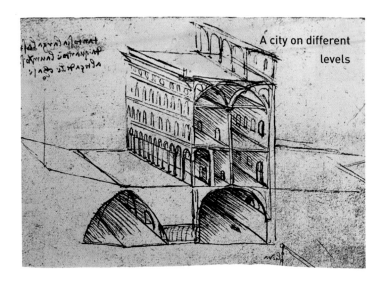

A city on different levels

circle of canals. Water was used in the fields and to move machines in workshops, and boats moved things around the city. Leonardo looked at the canals and studied how water moved through them. He designed moving bridges and new ways to use water wheels, and he designed canals that would work better and stay clean. Leonardo also wanted to build new canals from Milan to other places, like Pavia. In 1819, 300 years after he died, a canal was finished between Pavia and Milan, and Milan became one of the most important river cities in Europe.

Leonardo drew plans for a lot of buildings, like churches and castles. In 1506, he designed a house for Charles d'Amboise, the new ruler of Milan. There were two rivers near the house, so Leonardo designed two small canals to take water to a beautiful water garden in the house.

Many of Leonardo's designs were very modern for their time, and most of them were not built. In 1503,

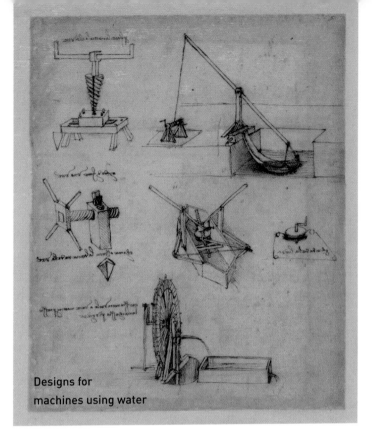

Designs for machines using water

Leonardo designed a bridge between the old city of Constantinople and Pera, in Istanbul. The bridge in his plan, 240 metres long, was bigger than any bridge in the world at the time. Leonardo's design for the bridge was very new, and people did not try to build bridges in that way for another 300 years. The Istanbul bridge was never built, but 500 years later, Norwegian artist Vebjørn Sand saw a drawing of the bridge and decided to build it. Finally, in 2001, a smaller 'Leonardo bridge' was built across a road in Norway. Now people are planning to build Leonardo bridges in Turkey, the USA, and other countries. Amazingly, in Des Moines, Iowa in the USA, people decided not to build a Leonardo bridge because the design looked 'too modern'!

7   A time of war

Everyone who wrote about Leonardo said that he was a kind man. He was good to his apprentices and he loved animals. So why did he work for dangerous men and design terrible war machines? How did he feel when he finally saw war for himself?

Many of Leonardo's inventions are war machines, and two of the most famous are called the 'machine gun' and the 'tank'. The machine gun drawings show lines of guns between two wheels. The guns shoot together, so they can kill a lot of soldiers at the same time. Leonardo's 'tank' was a metal machine with eight soldiers in it. The soldiers turned wheels inside the machine to move it, and they could shoot guns at the enemy outside. A few years ago, people built Leonardo's machine gun and tank for TV, and both machines worked.

In 1499, the French King Louis the Twelfth went to war, and his army took the city of Milan. Leonardo left Milan and travelled with a friend to Venice. When he arrived in 1500, Venice was fighting a war with the Ottoman Turks. Turkish ships and an army of soldiers waited in the Adriatic Sea, near Venice. People in the city were worried. How could they stop the Ottomans from taking Venice? Leonardo went to the rulers of the city with his ideas.

Leonardo planned some moving walls to stop the Turkish army at a river near Venice, and he also drew a boat which could go under the water. For another of his plans, Leonardo designed diving suits, 450 years before modern diving! Soldiers in diving suits could walk on the bottom of the sea, Leonardo explained, and make holes under the Turkish ships!

In the end, the Ottoman army never tried to take Venice – their ships sailed away to fight another battle. Nobody tried Leonardo's diving suit until a few years ago, when British diver Jacquie Cozens tried it on TV. After a small change to Leonardo's design, she walked on the bottom of the sea near Venice in a copy of the diving suit.

Between 1502 and 1503, Leonardo worked for Cesare Borgia – the most dangerous man in Italy. In two years of bloody battles, Borgia's army took cities all over the centre of Italy. Borgia was trying to build a new country for himself and his father. Leonardo travelled with him and helped Borgia to build better castles. There were terrible battles. For the first time, Leonardo learned what it really means to be a war engineer.

Cesare Borgia was a dangerous killer. He murdered a lot of his enemies – and some old friends. Leonardo left him very suddenly in 1503, and perhaps he left just in time!

The diving suit

Soon he was back in Florence. Florence was fighting a war with Pisa, and in June 1503, there was a terrible battle on a hill near Pisa. Soldiers from Florence took the castle on the hill, and a few days later, Leonardo arrived there. Could the castle be stronger? Leonardo's job was to look at the castle carefully and find ways to do this – before Pisa tried to take it back!

Cesare Borgia

Later, Leonardo and his friend, the writer Niccolò Machiavelli, had a good idea. Pisa got its water from the Arno River, and boats brought food into the city. So why not move the river? That way, Florence could win the war, and also become richer. The rulers of Florence loved their plans. Canals could take the river away from Pisa, and ships could sail along the canals to Florence, so the city would have a way to the sea.

In August 1504, thousands of workers began to cut the sides of the new canal. Leonardo designed machines to help, but he could not build them in time. In October 1504, there was a terrible storm. The sides of the canal fell away, eighty workers died, and the engineers went home. Once again, Leonardo tried to do too much.

8 The entertainer

The crowd laughs, cries, and shouts. Inside the theatre, mountains move, strange animals dance, and bright stars turn in the dark sky. When Leonardo planned parties and theatre performances for the court, they were nights of music, dancing, lights, and amazing surprises!

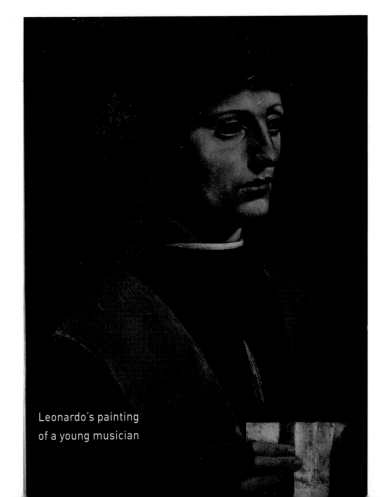

Leonardo's painting
of a young musician

A performance
at court

Leonardo did not just plan things – he was a great entertainer too. He told funny stories, and he was a very talented musician. When he first went to Milan, he was called 'Leonardo the musician', not 'Leonardo the painter'. He played musical instruments, and he sang as well.

Leonardo also wrote stories. They were often about animals, and they always had an important idea in them, like why we must be kind to other people. His stories were told in courts all over Europe, and when people told them, the stories slowly changed.

When Leonardo came into a room, everybody looked at him. He wore colourful clothes, he was very good-looking, and his hair was long when most men cut their hair short. Leonardo was funny, clever, and talented. By 1500, he was famous too. When Leonardo left Florence to visit Milan in 1506, the city's rulers did not want him to go. But the new French rulers of Milan wanted him to work there. For years, the two cities fought for Leonardo's time. The most important men of Europe wanted Leonardo, but what about his family?

When Ser Piero da Vinci died in 1504, he left houses and money to eleven of his twelve children. Leonardo got nothing. Many people in Leonardo's family did not have much time for him – or love. As a young child, Leonardo had to leave his mother Caterina to live with his father in Florence. He became very close to Ser Piero's first wife Albiera, but she died when he was young. After that, he was not close to many women, and he never married. In many ways, Leonardo's real family were his friends and apprentices: people like Salai, Zoroastro and Melzi.

Giacomo Caprotti was ten years old when he became an apprentice in Leonardo's workshop in 1490. He was soon in trouble. The other apprentices called him 'Salai', which means 'bad boy'. Salai said things that were not true and stole from people, but he became a talented painter. Over the years, he became one of Leonardo's closest friends.

Tommaso di Giovanni Masini, or 'Zoroastro', was good at working with metals. He started working with Leonardo in the 1490s. He kept strange animals and wore very unusual clothes. Neither Zoroastro nor Leonardo ate meat, because they did not want to kill animals for food. Zoroastro did not wear clothes that were made from animals either.

Some people think that Zoroastro tried to make gold from other metals. Today we know that this is not possible, but many people tried to do it in Leonardo's day. They worked in secret because it was a crime, and you could die for it. We can imagine Zoroastro in a workshop in the middle of the night. He is standing near the fire, doing dangerous work, and there is a smile on his face.

In 1507, Leonardo met a young man called Giovanni Francesco Melzi. Melzi came from a rich family, but like Salai, he became a painter in Leonardo's workshop. Leonardo was planning many books, and Melzi helped him to write his ideas. He followed Leonardo for the rest of the great man's life.

A painting by Melzi

9 Man of mystery

It was easy to invent stories about Leonardo. He had strange friends, he built moving robots, and he worked on dead people at night. His workshop was full of smoke and terrible smells. 'Is he trying to make gold?' people asked. 'Or to make living people from the dead?'

In 1513, Leonardo went to Rome to work for Giuliano de' Medici. Rome is the home of the Pope – the most important person in the Roman Catholic Church. The Pope at this time was Leo the Tenth, the brother of Giuliano de' Medici. Leo the Tenth was a very powerful man. He gave Leonardo a workshop, and some people to 'help' him. Leonardo did not know it, but he was probably in great danger. One of Leonardo's new helpers was telling the Pope about his work.

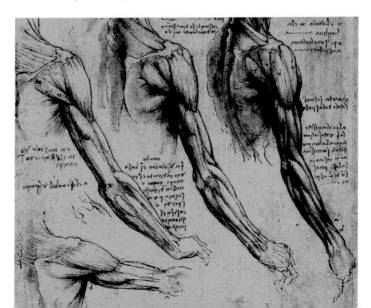

In 1514, the Pope's men took Leonardo's anatomy drawings and studied them. Many of Leonardo's ideas were different from the ideas of the Church. And at the time, people were killed because they did not agree with the Church. When the Pope told Leonardo not to study anatomy any more, he stopped!

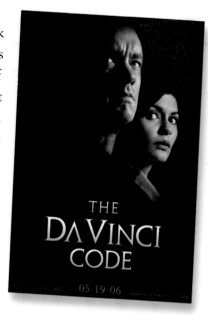

Leonardo's mirror writing was difficult to read. People like the Pope's men probably thought, 'What is he trying to hide? Is it a code?' The answer is probably that Leonardo wrote this way because it was easier for him. If you write with your left hand, it can be easier to write from right to left. But even today, people ask the same questions about Leonardo: 'What secrets did he know?'

Millions of people all over the world have enjoyed Dan Brown's book *The Da Vinci Code*. It tells the story of a secret code in one of Leonardo's most famous paintings, *The Last Supper*. Most people who study Leonardo's work say that *The Da Vinci Code* is just a great story, but are there any real codes in Leonardo's paintings?

In *The Last Supper*, Jesus and his followers are sitting at a table. You can see a lot of bread on the table, and a lot of hands too. In 2007, a computer engineer imagined

Opposite page: Drawings of arms by Leonardo

lines of music on the painting. He changed each hand or piece of bread into a musical note. When you read the notes from right to left – like Leonardo's mirror writing – it makes a short piece of music. Leonardo loved to play music and he probably wrote it as well. Did he put a musical code into the painting, or is it just an accident?

In November 2011, another possible code was discovered in the *Mona Lisa*. There are very, very small lines in the Mona Lisa's eyes and in other places in the painting. Some of these look like letters and numbers. For example, some people say that there is an L and a V in the Mona Lisa's right eye – perhaps for *Leonardo* and *Vinci*. But are these really letters, or lines that happen by accident when a painting gets older?

We know that Leonardo loved mysteries. In his paintings, he used things like trees or animals as codes for the name of a person. He also wrote mystery questions and drew picture codes to entertain people. If we look at his paintings again, will we find more secrets?

10 Leaving

One summer evening in 1515, hundreds of rich and important people were at a party in Lyon for François the First, the king of France. Suddenly, a door opened, and a robot lion came into the room. The lion moved its head and walked over to the king. Then a door in its body opened, and flowers came out. They were the *fleurs de lis*, the flowers of the kings of France.

The robot was a present from the Medici family to the new French king, and it was made by Leonardo da Vinci. The king liked this amazing present very much, and he

The robot lion

wanted Leonardo to come to France. After Giuliano de Medici died in March 1516, Leonardo stayed in Rome for a few months and then left. It was a good time to go. Younger painters like Raphael and Michelangelo were getting the best jobs in Rome, and the Pope's men were watching Leonardo.

In the summer of 1516, Leonardo rode across the mountains to France with his friend Francesco Melzi. He probably knew that he would never see his country again. Horses and other animals carried all of his things: his paints, paper and drawings, engineering models, books, and clothes. On the back of one animal, the *Mona Lisa* was carried across the mountains, through the rain and cold. The journey probably took them three months, and it was very difficult for Leonardo. He was old and ill, and he could not move his right hand any more.

When Leonardo arrived in France, François the First gave him a big house in Amboise, about one kilometre from one of the king's castles. There was a secret way under the ground from the castle to Leonardo's house. People say that the king visited Leonardo at night. The great old man from Florence and the young French king became great friends, and they talked for hours.

Leonardo probably did not paint in these years. He drew, wrote about engineering and science, designed buildings, and gave parties for the king. Famous people came to visit the great Leonardo, and look around his workshop. At the same time, he was working with Melzi and thinking about how to make his notes into books. He knew that he did not have much time.

Leonardo's home in Amboise

Leonardo da Vinci died on 2 May 1519. He was sixty-seven years old. In later stories and paintings, he dies in the arms of François the First, but we do not know if the king was really there at the time. Francesco Melzi was probably next to his bed, crying for his dear friend. Later, Melzi wrote a letter to Leonardo's family and told them of his death. Then he saved Leonardo's writings and kept them all his life.

In later years, Melzi's family sold and gave away many pages of Leonardo's work. Some of them were lost. Leonardo made over six thousand pages of notes and drawings about engineering, maths, anatomy, art, water, light, and many other things. But his notes were not made into books for a long time, so people could not learn from them. It took hundreds of years for other people to discover some of the things that Leonardo wrote about.

We are still finding lost work by Leonardo da Vinci today. Art detectives travel around the world looking for 'lost Leonardos'. They use the latest science to study

Leonardo da Vinci

hundreds of possible works, and sometimes they find a real one. In 1966, two books of Leonardo's notes and drawings were discovered in a library in Madrid, and in 2010, a note by Leonardo was found in France.

Then in November 2011, visitors to a museum in London stood in front of a Leonardo da Vinci painting called the *Salvator Mundi*.

The *Salvator Mundi* was painted by Leonardo in about 1513 for King Louis the Twelfth of France. Later, it went to Britain and then to America. For a long time people thought that it was by an apprentice called Giovanni Boltrafo, and in 1958 it was sold for only $70. In 2011, after years of study, the art world decided the painting really was by Leonardo da Vinci. If you want to buy it today, you need about $190 million!

11   A man who questioned everything

In 1977, an American pilot and sculptor called Charles Dent read about Leonardo's great horse sculpture. Dent decided to make the sculpture, and then give it to the Italian people. It took years for him to get the money, but finally sculptor Nina Akamu made two 8-metre horses. In July 1999, an Alitalia plane flew one of them to Milan. Once, Michelangelo laughed at Leonardo because he could not finish his horse, but Leonardo was right: the designs were good. At last, 500 years after French soldiers broke Leonardo's clay horse, the final sculpture stood in Milan.

Leonardo was right about another thing too: we have at last learned to fly!

Leonardo's horse in Milan

When we think of Leonardo today, we think of his art, his amazing inventions, and his many discoveries. But it is easy to forget that he was also a person, like us. Read his writing, and you will find the ideas of one of the cleverest people who ever lived – and notes about money, friends, and shopping!

Some things about Leonardo are not easy to understand. He was a great artist, but many of his paintings were never finished, and others broke into pieces. He was a scientist and inventor, but he hid many of his ideas. He was a kind man, but he worked for dangerous people like Cesare Borgia.

People tell a lot of stories about Leonardo, but some of them are not true. He could not see into the future. He did not really invent the car or the helicopter – his drawings are very different from those machines. Leonardo was not the only great man in Italy. There were other amazing artists, engineers, inventors, and thinkers in the Renaissance. But we remember Leonardo today because he was all of these things.

For all of his life, Leonardo asked questions and tried to understand the world around him. How can we make paintings more real? Where do fossils come from? What are things made of? How do birds fly? Why do we become old and die? Leonardo was a man who questioned everything.

Leonardo's last work was not a painting or an invention. It was a theatre performance for King François the First at Leonardo's house in Amboise. We can imagine that hot summer evening in June 1518. Lights are burning in the garden. The performance has finished, and people are

walking home. They have seen some amazing things, and they talk excitedly about the great man from Florence. Somewhere in the garden, an old man smiles, thanks people, and says good night. Then he walks away into the dark.

GLOSSARY

amazing very surprising

art beautiful things like paintings and drawings; **artist** a person who paints or draws pictures

artery one of the tubes in your body that carry blood away from your heart to other parts of your body

battle a fight between armies in a war

become to begin to be something

canal a long narrow passage that carries water

castle a large old building that was built in the past to keep people safe from attack

city a big and important town

clay a kind of heavy earth that becomes hard when it is dry

clean not dirty

code a way of writing secret messages with numbers or special signs

coin a piece of money made of metal

court the place where a ruler lives; a ruler, their family and the people who work for them

design to draw a plan that shows how to make something

discover to find or learn something for the first time; *(n)* **discovery**

draw to make a picture with a pen or pencil; *(n)* **drawing**

dream to hope for something nice in the future

engineer a person whose job is to plan or make things like roads or bridges; *(n)* **engineering**

entertain to do things that other people find interesting or funny

final last; **finally** after a long time

fossil part of a dead plant or animal that has changed to rock over a long time

good-looking nice to look at

heart the part of the body that makes the blood go round inside

history all the things that happened in the past

idea a new thought or plan; a picture in your head

imagine   to make a picture of something in your mind
instrument   a thing that you use for playing music
invent   to make something for the first time; *(n)* **invention**
level   a floor of a building, or a layer of ground
line   a long thin mark like this _____
machine   a thing with moving parts that is made to do a job
materials   what you use for making or doing something
maths   the study of numbers and measurements
metal   something solid that is usually hard and shiny; iron and
    gold are metals
model   a small copy of something
museum   a building where people can look at old or interesting
    things
musician   a person who makes music; **musical** connected with
    music
paint *(n & v)*   a coloured liquid that you put on things; **painting**
    a picture that somebody makes with paint; **oil paint** thick
    paint made with oil from plants
part   one of the pieces of something
performance   a time when a play is shown to a lot of people
pilot   a person who flies a plane
probably   almost certainly
problem   something difficult to understand, or find an answer for
robot   a machine that can work like a person
rock   something very hard that is found in the ground
ruler   a person who controls a country
science   the study of natural things; *(n)* **scientist**
sculptor   a person who makes shapes from things like stone or
    wood; *(n)* **sculpture**
study   to spend time learning about something
talented   having a natural ability to do something well
war   fighting between armies of different countries
workshop   a place where people make or repair things

ACTIVITIES

Before Reading

1 **Match the words to the pictures. You can use a dictionary.**

1 ☐ sculpture   3 ☐ workshop   5 ☐ battle
2 ☐ castle   4 ☐ paint   6 ☐ robot

2 **How much do you know about Leonardo da Vinci? Circle the correct words.**

1 Leonardo was born near Vinci in *1552 / 1452* .

2 Leonardo died in *France / Germany*.

3 The *Mona Lisa* is a famous *sculpture / painting*.

4 Leonardo invented *robots / trains*.

5 He was very good at playing *sport / music*.

ACTIVITIES

While Reading

Read Chapters 1 and 2, then choose the correct words to complete the sentences.

apprentice, artist, father, money, Latin, left, Renaissance, talented

1 Andrea del Verrocchio was a/an _____ in Florence.
2 Verrocchio was a friend of Leonardo's _____.
3 Leonardo's family did not have a lot of _____.
4 Leonardo could not read many books because he did not know _____.
5 Leonardo taught himself to draw and write with his _____ hand.
6 Leonardo became a/an _____ in Verrocchio's workshop.
7 Florence was a very important city in the _____.
8 There were many clever and _____ people in Florence.

Read Chapter 3, then put these sentences in the right order.

1 Leonardo made a great horse sculpture in clay.
2 Leonardo left Florence and travelled to Milan.
3 He planned a painting of a famous battle.
4 His father helped him to open a workshop in Florence.
5 Verrocchio realized that Leonardo was now a better painter than he was.
6 He started the famous painting *The Last Supper*.
7 The French army arrived and Leonardo left Milan.
8 The French army broke Leonardo's sculpture.

**Read Chapter 4. Choose the best question-word for these
questions, and then answer them.**

How / What / Where / Which / Who / Why

1 . . . did Leonardo go into a cave when he was a boy in
Vinci?
2 . . . did Leonardo find fossils of sea animals?
3 . . . things did Leonardo start to write about in Milan?
4 . . . famous drawing did Leonardo make in 1487?
5 . . . did Leonardo speak to in a hospital in Florence?
6 . . . did Leonardo's ideas help a doctor in England?
7 . . . was it difficult for Leonardo to study anatomy?

**Read Chapters 5 and 6 and match the sentences with
Leonardo's designs and inventions.**

*bridge, canal, helicopter, musical instrument, ornithopter,
parachute, robot car, water garden*

1 Leonardo made one of these from silver.
2 This worked like a clock and had three wheels.
3 A British man tested this in 2000.
4 A Russian boy invented this after he saw a drawing
by Leonardo.
5 This had wings that moved up and down like a bird.
6 Leonardo wanted to make this from Milan to Pavia.
7 Leonardo designed this for Charles d'Amboise's house
in Milan.
8 Leonardo wanted to build this between Constantinople
and Pera.

Read Chapter 7. Match the parts of the sentences, and then circle the correct words.

1 Leonardo designed a machine with soldiers in it . . .
2 He travelled to Venice with a friend . . .
3 Leonardo wanted to stop the Turkish army . . .
4 The Turkish army did not take Venice . . .
5 When he worked for Cesare Borgia, . . .
6 When Leonardo wanted to win a war with Pisa, . . .

a he drew plans for moving a *river / canal.*
b Leonardo designed better *castles / guns.*
c *after / before* the French Army arrived in Milan.
d by using soldiers with *diving suits / parachutes.*
e called the *machine gun / tank.*
f because their ships *lost a battle / sailed away to fight another battle.*

Read Chapter 8, then answer the questions.

1 What did people call Leonardo when he arrived in Milan?
2 How did Leonardo entertain people?
3 What did Leonardo look like?
4 What did Leonardo get when his father died?
5 Who was Leonardo close to when he was a child?
6 Why was Giacomo Caprotti called 'Salai' (bad boy)?
7 Which of Leonardo's friends was good at working with metals?
8 Who helped Leonardo to write his ideas?

Read Chapter 9. Are the sentences True (T), False (F), or not mentioned in the text (N)?

1 The Pope helped Leonardo to study anatomy.
2 Leonardo did not like one of his new helpers in Rome.
3 *The Da Vinci Code* is about a secret code in *The Last Supper*.
4 Leonardo wrote from left to right.
5 In Leonardo's time, a lot of artists used codes in pictures.
6 There may be very small letters in the *Mona Lisa*.

Read Chapters 10 and 11, then complete the sentences with names from the list below.

Nina Akamu / *Charles Dent* / *François the First* /
Leonardo / *Guiliano de Medici* / *Francesco Melzi* /
Michelangelo / *the* Mona Lisa / *the* Salvator Mundi

1 . . . died in 1516.
2 . . . travelled to France with Leonardo.
3 . . . went across the mountains on the back of an animal.
4 . . . became great friends with Leonardo.
5 . . . was a 'lost' work by Leonardo.
6 . . . read about Leonardo's horse sculpture and wanted to make it.
7 . . . made two 8-metre horse sculptures.
8 . . . once laughed at Leonardo because he could not finish his horse.
9 . . . was a man who questioned everything.

ACTIVITIES

After Reading

1 Use the clues below to complete the puzzle with words from the book. Then find the hidden 8-letter word.

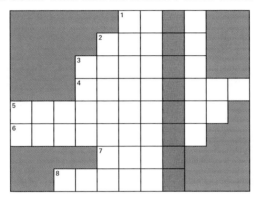

1 The most important person in the Roman Catholic church.

2 This is like a river, but people build it.

3 This animal or plant lived a long time ago, then slowly turned into stone.

4 A person who makes roads or bridges.

5 This plane has parts that turn. It can go straight up in the air.

6 To perform and interest people, e.g. by singing or telling funny stories.

7 A big, dangerous cat from Africa.

8 Swimming under the sea with oxygen.

The hidden word is _____.

My favourite (hidden word) _____ is _____ by _____.

2 **Complete the holiday advert with these words.**

apprentice, artists, born, buildings, drawings, gun,
instruments, models, paintings, sculptures, suit, workshop

Art Lovers' Italy:
Two-day da Vinci tour

Book now

Day 1: Vinci

On Day 1, we drive to Vinci, where Leonardo was _____. At the
Museum of Leonardo da Vinci, you will see many of Leonardo's
beautiful pen and pencil _____. The museum also has big _____
of many of Leonardo's inventions, such as his diving _____, a
machine _____ and some of his musical _____.

Day 2: Florence

Day 2 starts at the world-famous Uffizi Gallery, in Florence. Here
you can see work by Leonardo and by many of the greatest _____
of the Renaissance, from the beautiful colours of Raphael's _____
to Michelangelo's *David*, one of the world's most famous _____.
An afternoon walk will take you past the city's most important
_____, and we will visit Ghibellina Street, where Leonardo da Vinci
worked as an _____ in Andrea del Verrochio's _____.

3 **Find these dates in the book. Write a sentence about what happened on each date.**

1452, 1466, 1482, 1487, 1498, 1502, 1504, 1513, 1519

4 **Do you agree or disagree with these sentences? Why?**

1 Renaissance artists were more talented than artists today.

2 The *Mona Lisa* only became famous by accident.

3 Great people have very difficult lives.

4 Leonardo's ideas changed our world.

5 Leonardo's discoveries and inventions are more important than his art.

6 Nobody today could do all the things that Leonardo did.

5 **Write a short biography or give a talk to your class about an artist. Use websites like these to help you.**
http://www.wga.hu
http://smarthistory.khanacademy.org
http://www.louvre.fr (choose 'English')
http://www.nationalgallery.org.uk

Think about:

• the artist's life and the time when he/she lived.

• why this person became famous.

• how he/she changed the history of art.

ABOUT THE AUTHOR

Between 1991 and 1993, Alex Raynham worked as an English teacher in Italy. During those years, he had the chance to travel all around the country and see many of the greatest paintings and sculptures of the Italian Renaissance. One of his favourite memories of Italy was walking all night in the rain through the quiet, empty streets of Rome while he waited to catch a morning train. He remembers the lights on the beautiful buildings that night, and how their colours shone in the water of the wet streets.

Today, Alex lives with his wife Funda in the Turkish city of Adana, where he writes books for Oxford University Press, including graded readers. His other Oxford Bookworms Factfiles titles are *Formula One* and *Future Energy* (both Stage 3). In his free time Alex loves visiting art galleries, and he also paints. In the summer, you can often find him painting on a crowded beach in Turkey - often with a lot of people watching him!

OXFORD BOOKWORMS LIBRARY

Classics • Crime & Mystery • Factfiles • Fantasy & Horror
Human Interest • Playscripts • Thriller & Adventure
True Stories • World Stories

The OXFORD BOOKWORMS LIBRARY provides enjoyable reading in English, with a wide range of classic and modern fiction, non-fiction, and plays. It includes original and adapted texts in seven carefully graded language stages, which take learners from beginner to advanced level. An overview is given on the next pages.

All Stage 1 titles are available as audio recordings, as well as over eighty other titles from Starter to Stage 6. All Starters and many titles at Stages 1 to 4 are specially recommended for younger learners. Every Bookworm is illustrated, and Starters and Factfiles have full-colour illustrations.

The OXFORD BOOKWORMS LIBRARY also offers extensive support. Each book contains an introduction to the story, notes about the author, a glossary, and activities. Additional resources include tests and worksheets, and answers for these and for the activities in the books. There is advice on running a class library, using audio recordings, and the many ways of using Oxford Bookworms in reading programmes. Resource materials are available on the website <www.oup.com/bookworms>.

The *Oxford Bookworms Collection* is a series for advanced learners. It consists of volumes of short stories by well-known authors, both classic and modern. Texts are not abridged or adapted in any way, but carefully selected to be accessible to the advanced student.

You can find details and a full list of titles in the *Oxford Bookworms Library Catalogue* and *Oxford English Language Teaching Catalogues*, and on the website <www.oup.com/bookworms>.

THE OXFORD BOOKWORMS LIBRARY
GRADING AND SAMPLE EXTRACTS

STARTER • 250 HEADWORDS

present simple – present continuous – imperative –
can/cannot, must – *going to* (future) – simple gerunds ...

Her phone is ringing – but where is it?

Sally gets out of bed and looks in her bag. No phone.
She looks under the bed. No phone. Then she looks behind
the door. There is her phone. Sally picks up her phone and
answers it. *Sally's Phone*

STAGE 1 • 400 HEADWORDS

... past simple – coordination with *and*, *but*, *or* –
subordination with *before*, *after*, *when*, *because*, *so* ...

I knew him in Persia. He was a famous builder and I
worked with him there. For a time I was his friend, but
not for long. When he came to Paris, I came after him –
I wanted to watch him. He was a very clever, very
dangerous man. *The Phantom of the Opera*

STAGE 2 • 700 HEADWORDS

... present perfect – *will* (future) – *(don't) have to, must not, could* –
comparison of adjectives – simple *if* clauses – past continuous –
tag questions – *ask/tell* + infinitive ...

While I was writing these words in my diary, I decided
what to do. I must try to escape. I shall try to get down the
wall outside. The window is high above the ground, but
I have to try. I shall take some of the gold with me – if I
escape, perhaps it will be helpful later. *Dracula*

STAGE 3 • 1000 HEADWORDS

... should, may – present perfect continuous – *used to* – past perfect –
causative – relative clauses – indirect statements ...

Of course, it was most important that no one should see
Colin, Mary, or Dickon entering the secret garden. So Colin
gave orders to the gardeners that they must all keep away
from that part of the garden in future. *The Secret Garden*

STAGE 4 • 1400 HEADWORDS

... past perfect continuous – passive (simple forms) –
would conditional clauses – indirect questions –
relatives with *where/when* – gerunds after prepositions/phrases ...

I was glad. Now Hyde could not show his face to the world
again. If he did, every honest man in London would be proud
to report him to the police. *Dr Jekyll and Mr Hyde*

STAGE 5 • 1800 HEADWORDS

... future continuous – future perfect –
passive (modals, continuous forms) –
would have conditional clauses – modals + perfect infinitive ...

If he had spoken Estella's name, I would have hit him. I was so
angry with him, and so depressed about my future, that I could
not eat the breakfast. Instead I went straight to the old house.
Great Expectations

STAGE 6 • 2500 HEADWORDS

... passive (infinitives, gerunds) – advanced modal meanings –
clauses of concession, condition

When I stepped up to the piano, I was confident. It was as if I
knew that the prodigy side of me really did exist. And when I
started to play, I was so caught up in how lovely I looked that
I didn't worry how I would sound. *The Joy Luck Club*

BOOKWORMS · FACTFILES · STAGE 2
World Wonders
BARNABY NEWBOLT

What are the most beautiful, the most interesting, the most wonderful things in the world? The Great Pyramid, the Great Wall of China, the Panama Canal – everyone has their favourites. And there are natural wonders too – Mount Everest, Niagara Falls, and the Northern Lights, for example.

Here is one person's choice of eleven wonders. Some of them are made by people, and others are natural. Everyone knows the Grand Canyon and the Great Barrier Reef – but what about the Iguazú Falls, or the old city of Petra? Come and discover new wonders . . .

BOOKWORMS · FACTFILES · STAGE 2
Marco Polo and the Silk Road
JANET HARDY-GOULD

For a child in the great city of Venice in the thirteenth century, there could be nothing better than the stories of sailors. There were stories of strange animals, wonderful cities, sweet spices, and terrible wild deserts where a traveller could die. One young boy listened, waited, and dreamed. Perhaps one day his father and uncle would return. Perhaps he too could travel with them to great markets in faraway places. For young Marco Polo, later the greatest traveller of his time, a dangerous, exciting world was waiting . . .